sept

THE CITY OF
SATISFACTIONS

Daniel Hoffman

The City of

Satisfactions

NEW YORK

OXFORD UNIVERSITY PRESS 1963

Certain of these poems have appeared in *Approach, Carleton Miscellany, Columbia University Forum, Critical Quarterly* (England), *The Nation, Sewanee Review, Shenandoah,* and the anthology *Poet's Choice.* 'At the Winter Solstice' and 'As I Was Going to Saint-Ives' appeared originally in *The New Yorker;* 'A Letter to Wilbur Frohock,' 'Gestures,' and 'A Deliverance' in *Poetry.*

CONTENTS

I

At the Winter Solstice

Austerity is not asperity

as woodchuck and the snoozing owl
in oak's high hollow or blackberry root
sheltering feathered claw and fallow foot
against the winter's rude temerity
know well.

Then prosper them within the earthy hostel;

let time of icecaps and the soughing
hemlocks' sleet-sleeved pentecost
annunciate the coming of their host
in a risen guise again of the green gospel
at the sun's sowing.

A Meeting

He had awaited me,
The jackal-headed.

He from Alexandria
In the days of the Dynasts,

I from Philadelphia
In a time of indecisions.

His nose sniffed, impassive,
Dust of the aeons.

A sneeze wrenched my brain
—I couldn't control it.

His hairy ears listen
Long. He is patient.

I sift tunes from the winds
That blast my quick head.

His agate eye gazes
Straight ahead, straight ahead.

Mine watch clocks and turn
In especial toward one face.

I thank Priestess of Rā
Who brought us together,

Stone-cutters of Pharoah
And The Trustees of

The British Museum.
When with dog eared Anubis

I must sail toward the sun
The glistering Phoenix

Will ride on our prow;
Behind the hound-voices

Of harrying geese
Sink the cities of striving,

The fiefdoms of change
With which we have done,

Grown in grandeur more strange,
More heroic than life was

Or the dark stream at peace,
Or wings singed in the sun.

Climbing Katahdin

Hoisting yourself
From fingerniche to toehold,
Approaching the Knife-Edge,

A deep shagged ravine gapes on the one side,
The eye of a blueberry-silver pool steep
Down the dizzydrop other,

Your breath short,
Each rib rasping,
Grasping the thinned air above the timberline,

Clinging
To the desolate rocks
Below the snowline,

You can believe
As others have believed—
This stony ridgepole bracing

Heaven the longhouse of the mountain,
Ktaadn.
You breathe his breath.

Hoisting yourself
Atop the spined ridge you'll find
On a slight plateau

Stretching toward the peak's rise
Huckleberries growing
Beside a spring!—you laugh at the surprise

Of it and chew in the icy air
Bursting berries big as birds' eggs,
Your lips and tongue relish the purple—

Then arise from feasting
On silvery frosted fruit
In the desolation

To hoist yourself,
From fingergrip to tochold
Each breath grasping

As high up as the mountain allows you.

The Chosen

I am the one that drew
The black cake from the fire.
Then the sun throbbed
With blood's accusations.

Skulking fox and ferret snarl
In the dry rocks
At my tread.
Trees lock their arms against me.

The buzzard whose hover
Over the living
Spreads dread
Stills the wind above me

Whatever the track I follow.
Stones speak:
I have no fellows.
What did I do among them,

When, till this day
My lusts were young
And I lived as they live,
Bruising the earth,

That was worse than their wrongs
Or deserving their worst
Who last night lived as I lived
And now fling me forth?

The Unchosen

I didn't feel good
Even when I
Drew a white one. My blood

Beat like the toll
Of a bell in a blizzard.
Still ashake with fear's dole,

I watched him stand
Right beside me, and smile,
The black cake in his hand.

Then my belfry of bone
Nearly cracked out of pity
And—it missed me by *one*—

Joy. A stark stroke
Silenced the sun.
We stood still, stunned.

Then he cried out and broke
From our ring,
Ran alone, ran alone,

Raced up the heath.
As the sun oozed and bled
His lengthening

Shadow made dread
Hackle our marrow.
He grew with our dread

Til he was a shadow,
The gobbet that looms
On nightmare heath,

Presentiment of death
Committing our dooms,
Guilty of life.

We breathed the one breath,
Then with the one
Lunge, the one yell

We picked up stones.
We flung stones at its head.
The sun boomed like a bell—

We returned together.
We roasted the meat together.
We drank, we rejoiced together.

We were safe. We felt good.

The Exile

Why, the water rushed out of that hillside—
Mole tunnels burst,
Paths were runnels and roads rivers,
Turf became marsh-grass
And pebbles spun, glistening.
Silvery water streaked and flumed
Out of that hill.

Why does he linger splayfooted, wetshod,
Gauntly listening
As though the astringency of the rinsed air
Weren't pure enough,
As though the pungency of the pealed twitter
Of plover weren't,
Why, in a field of fountains, trying
To die of thirst?

In March

The bare trees bore the ruin of summer.
Ghost leaves groaned in windy arches.
Nests of ogres' wigs
Swayed in the crotches.

A scud of shadows and black foliage
From twig to twig with mantic purpose
Leapt—a rough croon
Of ravens in the larches,

Their bleak gossip of affection
Guttering in the wind. What omen's
In the wind's palaver
That norns like lovers mutter?

The Hill of Tara

Curled in the corner, writing
In her Nine-Year Diary
Her own sentiments,
Our itinerary

(The moist wind seemed
Desolation's breath
On the chilled ewes and rams.
On that feast-hall's fallen hearth

Where queens lie still, the wind
Pearled grey lichened earth.
A bare oak swayed and keened.
The thornbush, on that heath,

Mourned in tear-streaked beards
Of last year's tattered wool.
None but the New Year's
Lambs leapt on that hill)—

'On the Hill of Tara
I felt like dancing,
And then the wind seemed to sing
So I danced to the song of the wind.'

In That High House

In that high house half up a hill
A string linked your hand to my hand.
From the swollen sea that gnashed the shore
A road coiled round the hill's stone breast.
Our string pulls taut, frays, snaps apart.
The castle's ruined, a winter's tree.
You mustn't cry now, little son.
The rooftree's fallen and the moon
Through skeletal shadows lights the hall.
Beyond the broken door a road
Coils round the ridges of a hill
Where another house may stand
And your hand loop another hand
And when that filament frays and falls
In roofless walls remember us
When most together most alone.

Beyond the Mountain

Wherever we went, there was the mountain leaning
Gleaming toward us. Every valley slanted
Steeper upward as we came. Shoulders,
Knolled elbows, arms spread to enfold us.
The way to the flatlands glowing in the distance
That mountain's blazing glazed peak blocked,
A bonfire on a cairn we cannot come to
From spume and roothold, inescapable,
But at each approach add one more stone.
And should we find a crevice through the mountain
We'd be hard-pressed to once again remember
The way back to these crag-cool leafy valleys
Where streams plummet and the wild deer leap
Nor why, the golden glare of snow above us,
We struggled toward a dry plateau of craters
Where dust silts velvet the one shadow.

Natural History

If, at the bottom of the sea, the whales arrange
Collectanea of human relics,
Bones all barnacled and the hearts by those slow strange
Deeps coralled in their spiny cases
To show life's prolix range of norms and features
With lightning-eels to shine on the drowned faces
Set, in the brine, in the taut grimaces

Of creatures who enact their inmost natures,
What, then, could the educative sign
In whale-calligraphy on harpoon handle inked
Say but, 'This unfinned sport with little spine
Was fierce as froth asnarl on the crest of the surf is.
Habitat: Found only on the surface;
Tried beyond its depths to spout; believed extinct.'

Fables

If animals could talk would it depress us
To bear with noble horses' boring headaches,
Endure mendacities from nosey starlings,
And learn how frivolously the horned cow ponders
The cud that won't stay down, while the chameleon
Beneath an opportunistic skin
Holds unimpeachable faith with the one tenet,
That it is good to eat, and, with one eye
Half-creased asleep, sops up the heat of the sun?

If we could understand the animals would it inspire us
To be assured that kittens don't aspire to be
Lionesses? That bees who build domed cities
Are stupid and incapable of dreams?
That the groundhog doesn't give a damn for shadows,
And Æsop was a great prevaricator
Who made the creatures caper to the laws
The Greeks derived from Reason since observance
Danced less convincingly on toes than claws?

The Toad

'I was going home to dinner past a shallow pool
green with springing grass when it occurred to
me that I heard the dreaming of the toad.'
—Thoreau, *Journal,* 26 October 1853

You needn't think a back of warts condemns
My dreams to brood on envy. Every creature
Born of egg Sir Thomas Browne commends
Who wrote down, 'There are no Grotesques in Nature.'

Lulled in a canopy of arrowgrass
My gates of horn close on these dozing eyes.
The depths I come from clear, a waterglass
Creating truth in that it magnifies.

The wraiths aswirl there spell for my delight
Such fables of our rising out of silt
Toward slithery freedom, pure breaths of the light
Though smooth flesh wither into wart and welt,

That when the evening hints at wizened sleep
This sack of skin hung dewlapped from my jowels
Draws taut with breath as heady, long, and deep
As I can hold: a booming belch of vowels

Looses the ecstasy in my cool blood.
Whose is the excellence my song can mime?
—Pluperfect beauty in a pool of mud;
The jewel that's in my forehead is a dream.

Reading The Times

They must be different from us,
Those top persons
Whose indecisions and decisions numb us
As the time worsens;

Missile-to-missile construction booms,
The economy hearkens;
Thumpings are felt in many wombs
Though the milk darkens

—But 'Passive suffering is not a theme
For poetry,' cried Yeats
Who, touched by the Sidhe when young, could dream
That he creates

Exultant destiny once more as though
Homer had not
Used up all heroism long ago.
Still, what's to stop

Imagination, even now
Unreason's spawn, and power's, abuse our age?
If woe blast Paradise, or threat of woe,
Then, great with rage,

Turn, Imagination, and conceive
On days like dragons' teeth.
What can be brought to birth but we bequeath
The primal gift

Of where we've been and have to go?
Then in that deed
Play out, as ever we'd the will to do,
The natal thread—

Retell, in the leaping of exultant breath,
In the blood that sighs,
What knowledge in the bone this side of death
Death makes us prize.

II

Saint-Apollinaire

September sunlight,
apples in the baskets,
potatoes in the bins,
rabbits in the barn,
cordwood under the outside stairs,
a tile-topped chimney lisping woodsmoke
pungent in the evening air,
odor of apples seeping through the floorboards,
nightlong dried-earth smell of the potatoes,
furtive skitters in the darkness,
mousefeet in the bins,
mice along the rafters,
snug in the farmhouse,
live coals in the grate the whole night long.
Dew stiffens gelid grass leaves.
Steps crunch the pebbly path
bringing bread in the morning,
morning bread
to Saint-Apollinaire.
We push dark shutters outward.
Their rims dazzle in lightfalls pouring
over the windowsill in splashes
awash on the scrubbed tiles.
The children in their smocks are singing
their schoolward way among the asters.

Dijon

In November they pollarded the plane trees,
   bound the branches into besoms,
     stacked faggots
to dry through half the winter by the wall.

Our Katy cried to see those amputees
   bear wintry rime on clumps of stumps
     like veterans of wars,
undecorated files at crooked rest.

The empty sleeve-men, one on a leg of pole,
   hump their ways among the plane trees
     in crooked ranks
as Maquis infiltrate the guarded flanks

of courts, and vanish in a clank of gates
   to warm the marrow of their wounds
     at hissing hearths
where lopped branches redly singe and sigh.

When woodsmoke lifts from the Place de la République
   and air between the walls grows clearer
     the lined trees,
rainwashed familiars of paucity, remain,

Their knobs aswell with nodes of summer's verdure
   as though time and the sun could nurture
     and eke a future
of live limbs tousling the wind from every suture.

Vezelay

Preach me no preachments John Ruskin
of the Aspiration of pointed Arches,
of the 'wing'd nobility' of buttresses.
I have voyaged over waters for the laving of my sight.
I have found a still font
where, in the amber twilight
from column to column the arches
leap, and the light hallows
the curvature of hollows
the rhythm of the columns
the anthems of the silence
ethereal masses. Heaven's
obsidian light pours down
on the joyous Doomsday
of Christ and the creatures
the zodiac of vintners
the sacrifice of oxen
the dogheaded devils
peoples of the earth.
Our sins upon the capitals
breathe in rippling light,
move in the fluent light,
move in their own commission
till in the mind this moment
turns stone,
stone in the mind carved
with devildogs and virgins
butchering the ox in

stone relief, the drunken
vintners in the mind's eye
stony-eyed, the creatures
of the mind arrested,
gargoyle imagination's
personae held in stone
carven on the capitals
under rippling vaultribs
dancing down the arches.
Each in the absolute
joy of strict proportion
leaps from stone to stone
image of the earthfolk,
image of this moment
carved in the mind,
all dooms dancing
toward that stone Resurrection:
Breath on the Tympanum.

1956

That week the fall was opulent. Vendanges,
  Dancing, sunlight, autumn warmth, full larder
  Before the endurable oncome of the winter.

Needing a haircut, I asked the coiffeur again
  To cut it short. He shrugged, but, being genial,
  Complied. A Samson came in for his marcel.

Musique à la radio cut short: Shrill voice:
  Our fleet en route to liberate Suez!
  Nasser, beware! Victory in two days!

Then glory used up all the largest type fonts
  As Napoleonic ghosts in parachutes
  Converged canalward on those camel-troops.

Coiffeur and Samson were ready for the glory.
  But Egyptians, seeing Israel's guns, skedaddled
  Before the Indo-China vets embattled

Them. The RAF pounded the desert
  For two days. Meanwhile John Foster Dulles
  (My countryman) put through long distance calls

To God again, and passed The Moral Law
  Again. Texas and Oklahoma cheered
  His oil on troubled waters. It appeared

OK to Moscow too. Peace took the UN
   By unsurprise. Beaten yet once again,
   Dienbienphu yet unavenged, Pétain

Yet unavenged, Verdun . . . My hair grew longer.
   I went to the coiffeur again. This day
   In short supply I found l'amitié.

I spoke of soccer, not Suez, nor glory.
   His shears yet jabbed my head most dangerously.
   The next man up read 'Combat' sullenly.

L'amitié is scarce. A run on soap.
   Hoarders have got the rice. There's no coal
   In the coalyards. At the school, no oil;

What's plenty? A pyramid in the Magasin
   Of canned-for-America grapefruit, tin on tin;
   A sign says: 'PAMPLEMOUSSES ISRAËLIENS.'

The ration of gas threatens the Cabinet.
   Canal-boats on the Ouche fray weedy hausers.
   Nobody mentions glory now, or the Gaza,

But curses the malign sphinx of history.
   By the Arc de Triomphe they await who'll unriddle the past
   And may, even now, be descending the mountain path.

A Letter to Wilbur Frohock

ST-APOLLINAIRE (CÔTE D'OR)

NOVEMBER, 1956

Cher Maître:

Neither my explication
of 'Le Dernier Abencérage'
nor the almost-fluency
at quip and badinage

attested by your A minus
a decade ago
in 'Oral Intermediate
French' suffices now;

a beret is not enough.
Je puis acheter du pain
mais, when I go to the coalyard
as I do, again and again,

my first word or gesture's
carte d'identité,
sufficient proclamation:
'JE SUIS ÉTRANGER.'

'Sell you coal? My poor mother
Burns faggots in her mountain hovel—
You've la bombe atomique in your country—
Our children go barefoot in winter'

29

la marchande rails, distrait—
Besides, her coalyard's bare;
but, as you've said, the structure
—impeccable—of their

grammar reflects the logic
of the French mind. We've been here
two months. By now the neighbors
say 'Bonjour, Monsieur';

in our village there are two eggs
for sale each second day,
reserved for the toothless aged
or a sick bébé

and when our boy got queasy
and couldn't take his meat
at l'épicerie they sold me
un oeuf for him to eat—

My accent's improving.

Gestures

Before train-time they swept across the track
Bare-headed or beretted, in a tide
   Bearing loaves
Of *pain d'épice,* bottles of Nuits-St-George
And Chambertin. The engine nudged a furrow
Across their crest and chuffled to a stop.
   They thrust the loaves and bottles

Of the best they had to give toward open windows
Where, bleared and grizzled, the late triumphant hosts
   Of Budapest
Outstretched their hands in pauperage and pain
And pride. *Vive la liberté! Vive
La liberté!* chanted the crowd. The few
   With French enough replied

'Merci' for Dijon's gifts of gratitude,
Of homage to their hopeless hope, of guilt
   That others died,
That others fought and fled, their future left
Behind, that boy propped on a hard-backed bench,
A swollen bullet in his throbbing arm,
   While we communed with *pain*

D'épice and *premiers crûs*. The engine, watered,
Whooshed and strained. The stock began to roll
   Toward the mountains:
A disused camp for Prisoners of War
Would roof them in while squat Red tanks patrol
All homeward roads past Austria. Then peace
   Settled from grimy skies

As a wild gull, daubed in coaltar, flounders
Disconsolately down to a joyless rock.
   In bitter weather
We heard that some escaped Hungarians,
One with a sling, from Dole toiled up the Juras
Toward the immaculate freedom of that zone
   That looms in Alpine snow.

Mi-Carême

We were surprised by Mi-Carême's obtruding
On half the acerb season, when the fishes'
Trials of frailty almost seemed habitual.
A small renunciation of the flesh is
A thorn, though not in truth a crown, until
What's done without no longer pricks regret.
Well, on the rue de la Liberté that day
The breeches' bulge, the gaygrin becks all told
In winks of mask what fireworks stuttered out:
The feast of frivol's come, beneath the gaze
Of Jacquemaire, who, steeple-tall, emerged
At the booming sennet of his hourly bells.
Such images as these helped to dispel
Almost all trace of Lenten abnegation
In resurrections of the corpse interred
At Mardi Gras:
                          Those monsters at Chalon
Had made incomparable mirth. Some strode
On longlegs teetering past the crowded eaves;
A pair of osier giants, heads like eggs
The last roc laid before the earth grew cool,
In couthless courtship dipped and ducked and danced,
Joy's colossi, rathe for ridicule.
Tunes tattered the air festooned with flags then
As instrumental joculators wove
In sinuous undulations in between
His lumbering ankles and the porte-cochère
That a nest of pulleys held in her skirts aloft.

Now green snow fell, turned paper in our hair
As La Reine des Roses in her sheen negligée
Floated on a swan afloat on streams
Of streamers, bobbing heads and foams of sound.
Then fezzed trombonist, houri tambourine,
Libidinous flügelhorn and urgent drum
Conducted onward all these orotund
And liberal-featured figments of our glee
Beyond the turret-portals of the city
With peals of jubilation, casting them
To exile in a wilderness of marshes.
On tabletops, from our café, we leaned toward
Their unabated pantomime, their sway
To inaudible rhythms as the wind returned
An intermittent summons from the river.
There, across the high bridge to the island
A grave tribunal of the bishopric
Attended, palled in funeral pomp, and poised
To cinder all that gaiety in the end.

At Mi-Carême they dance before me still,
Made midget by the distance, silhouettes
Moving mirrored over the sheen of Saône,
Their procreant gestures ravelling sky and water
With earth till purification of the flame.
Now false-faced gamins shake their clipper-clappers
Against the Lenten rectitude, remembering
The boil of blood, the surge of seed, the sensual
Plentitude before the human legend
Recalls us to supernal imitation
And the weights of sorrow under the haloed sun.

III

A New Birth

When I was brimmed inside the shell
Sun and lion's mane
Were my near familiars.
Sheep and turtle came;
Heron cradled the nest—
O all the creatures covered me
With warm breast.

While I turned in a warm cocoon
Man and Rome fell.
Furrows scarred the valleys.
Haggle, blow and toil
Echoed at the stony gates,
Yet discipleship to the seasons
Made gay the festival.

All that long labor made me
Who split my earthling skin
In a fallen wind, a dusty sky.
What patrimony I come by
Lies, an empty sack,
Shrivelled fables at my back.
This is a new birth I begin.

The Arrival

They burdened him, even though duty-free,
His Father's bags. So did the oldtime guide-
Book that weighed one down. It seemed nobody
Used that dialect these days in this town
That towers too high for any human need.
Some things his Pa had said though did prove wise
—Precepts recalled too late as he strolled down
The wharf, his pockets and valise picked clean.
Thus unencumbered, feet on solid ground,
Remembered caravels that came to find
A different land from what in fact they'd found.
Agape at topless towers, he set his mind
To reckon what he'd come to find or found.

His Own Man

Boards, nails, staples, lengths of rope
And tools were issued to them all. They toiled
In the scorch of sawdust to a yelp of hammers
Making boxes, as was requisite,
With leg-holes; rope straps hung them from their shoulders
And as they marched all whistled the one tune.
One was there who chafed at this till galls
From boards the same fit as his fellows' boards
Bruised his shinbones. Craftily he schemed
To toil: By chops of clever saw and hammer
Made his box octagonal while walking.
Next, toothed a different tune. Now hopped upon
The left foot twice, in individual pace.
Then, as he looked about, he was surrounded
By octagons that kept his step and whistle.

Pin-Ball

Better than motorbikes, this tensile fusion.
Nerves and body staked, exploding balls
Blinding jaggle of lights in a throbbed jungle
Where bumpers bash brash bells and numbers
Spin to score the potent hipbone:
He leans against the glass-cased simulacrum
In motion moving with the hard pellet.
It's boredom, boredom, the incubus that's flapping
Beyond the neon in the swollen dark
While bells burp and lights bark and pale flippers
Heave and heave against the electric scoreboard
All purposed strength this side the sign marked 'Tilt.'

O Sweet Woods

Down my most tangled paths of revery
A man with a transistor radio walks.
Sweet are thy woods, o solitariness;
This stranger with convivial Rock-box gawks
In mine. He comes alone, strolls unbefriended,
By vibraharps' pubescent plaints attended.
Full-ON reception blurs the voice that talks.

Surfeit with speech, I'd drink in strength from silence
Anonymous in a crowd. But me he stalks,
Nor rests to skew my solitariness.
Past network's blare all his reception baulks;
How could he bear the hush that I intended?
Such paucity unended must be ended—
Full on my revery's assassin walks.

The Solid Citizen

He lived in a suburb he worked in a branch
Of a suburb a suburb a branch of a branch.
Partitions of grass and hedgerows of glass
Interposed on his days an insular glaze
So the fonts that hurled at his morning eye
Howling the hugeness of history
Gnashed and mumbled in other tongues.
On a day when he went to the center City
His arclit shadow stretched empty streets
Watched by windows, menaced in whispers
Stuttered from flags on rhetorical winds.
In the morning the Bulletin told of decisive
Intrigues, of mobs that massed at the crossings,
Uprisings downthrowing regimes in the flexion
Of power—the type spelled his hometown.
Barricades sprouted like bulbs in his absence.

A Late Spring

(PARIS, 1962)

Citizens stroll, irrelevantly.
Guardsmen walk in threes
Warily, at the ready
Cradling carbines. Trees

Disguise the Spring mourning
With thin green veils of broom.
Where three roads come together
Wreaths may sprout from stone;

Where three roads join two gypsies,
A monkey and a bear
Chant an antique hymn and dance now
To a skin tambour.

Conspirators, behind the statues,
Hold chaos in a bag;
The bear in dancing circles
Keeps seasons on their track.

Three soldiers round each corner
And they know what to do,
Ordered by their Orders;
The monkey capers too

And barred windows open
And children fling coins down
And the long frost is broken.
The old tableau moves on,

A new one waits its turn.
Shutters clang tight-barred.
On moon and leaf and sun's the stain
Though cobbles be fresh-scoured.

The Pursued

Surely he'd outwitted them, outdistanced them and earned
Respite at this café. There goes the ferry.
Two trips risked in his own person, over
And back, and now, in this wig
Crossed again. Nobody knew him.
Coffee under the arbor, mission done,
Content. And then he recognized
The first signs—
Heat, hotter than the day's heat, swarming
And his skin parched, stretching
Tight about each finger; the eyes
Pounding: arbor, harbor,
Table, gable, all begin to swing
Up and forth, forth and up, up and so, until
Giddily earth grinds beneath him, shudders;
Sweat oozes icy on his neck now,
On shaking chest a shirt of seaweed crawls,
Iron table rat-tat-tat-tat-tats against his elbow
Though harbor's calm and arbor's still. You've seen
A stepped-on centipede left on the pavement,
Each limb's oracular gesticulations?
—Cutting through the scent of pear trees
Klaxons, baying, toil up up the highroad,
Vans of his other pursuers.

IV

The Line

It was of first essentiality
To stand on line,
To take one's place
At the tail of the long serpentine
Assemblage among strangers
And see, behind one, strangers coming
To take their places at the tail
Of the serpentine assemblage
That slowly shrivelled toward its head
Around the corner.
Some stood in line with stoical
Glum resignation,
Some fidgeted, some wagged
In lively conversation;
Intimacies sprang up
But time would not be killed
And the line was long.
When my time came I turned
The corner we had inched up on.
There was no one behind me.
I turned again: No corner.
I stood, a stalk of flesh
Midway between the ringed horizons
An empty desk
A vacant chair.
It was of first essentiality
To wait on line,
To take one's place among the strangers
In serpentine assemblage
That shrinks toward its own head.

The City of Satisfactions

As I was travelling toward the city of satisfactions
On my employment, seeking the treasure of pleasure,
Laved in the superdome observation car by Muzak
Soothed by the cool conditioned and reconditioned air,
Sealed in from the smell of the heat and the spines
Of the sere mesquite and the seared windblast of the sand,
It was conjunction of a want of juicy fruit
And the train's slowdown and stopping at a depot
Not listed on the schedule, unnamed by platform sign,
That made me step down on the siding
With some change in hand. The newsstand, on inspection,
Proved a shed of greyed boards shading
A litter of stale rags.
Turning back, I blanched at the Silent Streak: a wink
Of the sun's reflection caught its rear-view window
Far down the desert track. I grabbed the crossbar
And the handcar clattered. Up and down
It pumped so fast I hardly could grab hold it,
His regal head held proud despite the bending
Knees, back-knees, back-knees, back-knees propelling.
His eyes bulged beadier than a desert toad's eyes.
His huge hands shrank upon the handlebar,
His mighty shoulders shrivelled and his skin grew
Wrinkled while I watched the while we reeled
Over the mesquite till the train grew larger
And pumping knees, back-knees, we stood still and
Down on us the train bore,
The furious tipping of the levers unabated
Wrenched my sweating eyes and aching armpits,

He leapt on long webbed feet into the drainage
Dryditch and the car swung longside on a siding
Slowing down beside the Pullman diner
Where the napkined waiter held a tray of glasses.
The gamehen steamed crisp-crust behind the glass.
I let go of the tricycle and pulled my askew necktie,
Pushed through the diner door, a disused streetcar,
A Danish half devoured by flies beneath specked glass,
Dirty cups on the counter,
A menu, torn, too coffeestained for choices, told
In a map of rings my cryptic eyes unspelled
Of something worth the digging for right near by
Here just out beyond the two-door shed.
The tracks were gone now but I found a shovel,
Made one, that is, from a rusting oildrum cover,
A scrap of baling wire, a broken crutch,
And down I heaved on the giving earth and rockshards
And a frog drygasped once from a distant gulley
And up I spewed the debris in a range
Of peaks I sank beneath and sweated under till
One lunge sounded the clunk of iron on brass
And furious scratch and pawing of the dryrock
Uncovered the graven chest and the pile of earth downslid
While under a lowering sky, sweatwet, I grasped and wrestled
The huge chest, lunged and jerked and fought it upward
Till it toppled sideways on the sand. I smashed it
Open, and it held a barred box. My nails broke
On the bars that wouldn't open. I smashed it
Open and it held a locked box. I ripped my knuckles
But couldn't wrest that lock off till I smashed it
Open and it held a small box worked

In delicate filigree of silver with
A cunning keyhole. But there was no key.
I pried it, ripped my fingers underneath it
But couldn't get it open till I smashed it
Open and it held a little casket
Sealed tight with twisted wires or vines of shining
Thread. I bit and tugged and twisted, cracked my teeth
But couldn't loose the knot. I smashed it
Open and the top came off, revealing
A tiny casket made of jade. It had
No top, no seam, no turnkey. Thimblesmall
It winked unmoving near the skinbreak
Where steakjuice pulsed and oozed. I thought aroma
Sifted, thinning till the dark horizon
Seemed, and then no longer seemed, a trifle
Sweetened. I knelt before
A piece of desert stone. When I have fitted
That stone into its casket, and replaced
The lid and set that casket in its box,
Fitted the broken top and set that box within
The box it came in and bent back the bars
And put it in the chest, the chest back in the hole,
The peaks around the pit-edge piled back in the pit,
Replaced the baling wire and crutch and oildrum cover
And pushed back through the diner, will the train
Sealed in from the smell of heat and mesquite
Envelop me in Muzak while it swooshes
Past bleak sidings such as I wait on
Nonstop toward the city of satisfactions roaring?
If I could only make this broken top
Fit snug back on this casket

52

A Deliverance

Striving over tortuous trails, we come to
A clapboard oldtime Opera House
Past ticket-taker down a wooden corridor
Toward the opening of the light from two high windows.
It's a room with benches. A door clicks behind.
Trapped in the room now, and the windows giving
On a steep drop down.
A stream unfurls below in silver tumbling.
From here there's no way out, and we've our mission
Still to do, rattling the locked doorjamb. . . .

I've come to redress wrongs. You will agree
It is disgraceful that the Library Staff
Of Aeronautical Sciences should dress
In eyepatches and pantaloons
To waylay travellers with promises
And keep men from their business in locked room?
With awed apologies he led me on inspection.
His staff leapt to attention as we came.
I saw the ones: That white-faced man, myopic,
With the pimples, and the other
Barrel-chested with a sneer around the eyes.
This one smirked and that one quailed to see me
State my charges to the colonel.
The staff was singing now, festive chorale
In Saturday night at the Yacht Club burst and gusto
As we stalked past their tables through a hall
That opened to a room with two high windows.

Behind the click of doors their singing stopped.
The windows gave out on a sheer drop down.
Below, a clittering stream unpurled in silver light.
'Why not come in my car?' said the colonel.
In the dark I placed my newspaper
Beneath the rear wheel on the snow—
'For better traction.' I turned the front door handle.
'You'll sit in back,' he said. The doors, I noticed,
Were hinged to open forward, as in old cars.
We were rolling when I saw
My Grandfather slide in beside him stiffly
Wearing a Panama. He said no word.
We swerved in silence through the darkness.
No headlights down this road.

Sometown

Past populated boardwalks beaches linger
Where fringed cabanas tempt the voluptuous sea.
Far factories scratch the inland sun,
Smudge the sun, smear a dying wind.
The road sweeps from this seaside and we follow
Around a turning
Colonnades a market square:
Today's no market day. Late afternoon
Isosceles triangles of dimmer shade
Lean against the towers. A thousand windows
Snatch uninhabited fletches of the sky
Brokenly reflected. Cobblestones
Reverberate down alleys of closed doors
Shuttered boulevards
Crossroad. Echoes surge and roar.
Solitary all in black a woman
Drags her shadow uphill on a stick.
This city
Has no suburbs only sheds
Walls switching yards deserted by the light
In the outskirts now the night
Sifts vacancy
Over the marshes. Tall distant windows
Glimmer through thickening shade.

In Hot Damp

Walls sweat,
Froths of mould
Sprout from cellar stones.
Fecund air hangs
Moist, a heavy breath,
Matted greenstuffs spreading,
Curling unabated
In the windless
Hot damp.
Distraction of the locusts
Resounds in the noon heat,
Crickets' incantations
Obliterate all echoes
Of remembered consolations,
Of the dry scrunch remembered
Of boots on drifts of powder
Swirling unabated
In the brittle wind
When walls cracked
And stones split
And eyes
In the spectral blue harsh snowlight
Ached
For the green,
For the warmth
Of now.

The Great Horse Strode Without a Rider

The great horse strode without a rider.
He looked as though no bit had ever reigned him,
No girthstrap squeezed the gloss of his firm belly.
The glass store windows mirrored him in broken
Images he smartly paced between.
His hooves precisely clapt upon the pavement.
Pistol-shots sound like his taut tattoo.
Pedestrians in ant-swarms elbowed doorways
Crouched beneath his image in the glass
On Commerce Avenue, until he came
To where it broadens under aisles of trees.
Now he was trotting and the trees dropped shadows
Flicking on and off his flanks in ripples.
His jaunty nostrils gathered all the wind in
That strained through sweetened lindens. Now he breathed
An easy laboring while criss-crossing feet
Rapped sharp *accelerandos*. In the houses
Watchers dropped their gaze from square glazed cages
To caress his rump. Then he was gone,
Past the furthest gatehouse by the roadside
Where roadsides run to thistles in the daisies,
And I though not astride him yet beside him
Moving with like movement to his speed
Now watch him break into a frolic canter.
His capers kick the clods up leaping after.
Now breasting upward toward the wind he gallops.
His mane whips like the backlash of sea-breakers

Over the ridge while I'm still struggling upward
Over the ridge. He's running down the headland.
He's far beyond me now and yet I see him
In clarity beyond the meed of sight.
His mighty movements pull me as the moon
Toward the vast intensity of heaven
Tugs the laggard tides. He's poised there, leaping
To for an instant hang as the hawk hangs, plunge then
Forefeet stretched to part the weedy froth
And disappear below the hill's rock brow.
Laboriously I clambered down the cliffside,
Pushed my way through wave-smashed bluffs past tide-pools,
Came at last to the broken stone declivity
Where spittled breakers, foam on rippled chests
And heads wind-tossed in their relentless oncome,
Lunged out of the sea to heave before me
The hugeness of their purpose, on, and on,
In charge on echoing charge against the shore.

Fledglings

Where there's a barn facing the sea,
A door blown down, the square hole gaping
And haymounds settle pocked with salt
In the cool shade and sweetening dung,
By the rusting waggon we lay down.
The golden giddy blaze of noon
That crackled in the huckleberry bushes
And shrivelled snails left high by tidefall
Roared beyond our weatherboarded walls.
The children dozed in our laps, and we
Drowsed deep beneath those shady eaves.
It was the twittering made us start and
Turn as though the beams were crying
A shower of sibilants in diminished light—
Then, in the gabled gloom, we saw them
Skittering urgent pirouettes:
There, on thimble-nests beneath the rafters
Bleated teetering swallows, black-lamblike,
Little and scared at the nests' edge. Under
Their bobbling heads the big ones (half a handspan)
Spun such nets of flight that all could leap
Assured into that shaft of space a thousand
Birdheights from the speckled floor.
One by one hove skinny pinions
Flapping frantic in the swirl of motes
Till stretched-out claws gripped, splinter-tight,
The next tier down of rafters. We gaped while
Elders looped-the-loop, exhorting, praising

The runtiest beak-faced bird that fluttered
Toward the shade-line on the fallen door.
Beyond, on the pulsing light of open sky
Swallows tumbled in miraculous freedom,
Whirling on forked tails in the glowing air.
On knobby knees the last bird leaned and leapt up—
He's flying! Two by two, the swallows
Cross, criss-cross beneath him. Invisible threads
Support and pull him toward the low bough
Of the apple tree. The barn is empty,
Their echoes fade among the dust-motes,
Broken shells and droppings, mouldering hay.
—Break free,
Lunge into the thickening light—
In swift leaps and jets of laughter
Our children on the border of the water
As saltimbanques of the air
Flash in joyous flight.

V

Three Jovial Gentlemen

Three jovial gentlemen
   Arriving with the dawn,
Down, down the mountain
   A-hunting they have gone.

One has brought a bag of salt,
   One a net of thongs,
Another a bow and arrow's brought.
   The taut cord thrums.

They've taken the pleasure of their craft
   In kenning and in cunning,
For the five full hours sun swelled aloft
   Kept the morning running.

Their manly mettle they've shown when
   Astride through bourne and byre
The unremitting afternoon
   Smote them with breaths of fire.

The evening's slunk in purple pall
   At their undaunted coming,
Net still empty, sack still full,
   And the bow-cord thrumming.

Night that's nipt their knuckles raw
   And smudged their clean-limned eyes
Some say surprised them on the hill.
   Some say 'twas their surprise.

Hapless, they've disarmed them, then
    Lain down to snatch their rest.
If the same dream's dreamt by several men,
    Three by one fate possessed,

Whether those wings were white or jet,
    Of metal, flame or feather,
Those three hunstmen even yet
    Asseverate together

They've heard in her voice the peal and dole
    Of the moon and the deep tide's timbre
Gong and toll on the shell of their soul
    And their pulse rings out, 'Remember,

'Who hunts me by thought's glazened glare
    Toils to snare a shadow,
Who cleaves the dark around my bower
    Wayward as joy's arrow
Serves and masters all my power
    With incandescent marrow.'

Three jovial gentlemen
    Are rising in the dawn.
Down, down the mountain
    They hunt on, and on.

Ballad of No Proper Man

As I was going down the lane
And my love's hand holding my hand
I met a man, no proper man
With a turn and a caper on the sand.

'She will come with me,' he said,
'I'll take your love's hand in my hand.
You can wither in a narrow bed
And I will caper on the sand.'

'I will not let my love leave me,
I'll hold her hand close in my hand
Until the tide empties the sea
For all your capers on the sand;

'My love stays here by my right side,
Her hand holds fast within my hand
Till the last sprig on the yew has died
Though you tumble on the sand,'

I cried defiance in his teeth
Who clasped my love's hand in his hand.
Cold was the wind that clenched my breath
And skittered across the gritty sand.

Yesterday the waves lunged high
When my love's hand held to my hand.
The hollow deeps are stony dry.
Who is that capers on the sand?

Last night the green fields sucked the dew
When my hand cleaved to my love's hand.
The wind now rattles a withered bough
And turns and capers on the sand.

My love my love where are you gone
Who held my hand tight in your hand?
My heart shakes bars of narrow rib-bone.
Who is that capers on the sand?

The True Testament of Thomas the Rhymer

I heard her singing,
Voice like a fire in a wineflask,

I stepped into the circle where
She sang in the dark of the dolmens,

I remembered the admonitions
That chilled chimney corners and churches,

I remembered the slender curve of her
Waist and her hips' sudden burgeon,

I lay down between the dolmens
Dark as tombs in the moon's lack,

I held her in my arms close,
I took from her the fruit of the darkness

That binds my bones to her will.
Now I cannot remember

What I did when I had a will,
I cannot remember any longer

What I did when I had a soul
But wander from moonless to moonless

Crossroad, a lack-love driven
To stumble through rockpit and furze

In an aching shadow imprisoned
Till all my fivewits serve her;

I have eaten the fruit of the darkness
And am freed thereof

To lie seven years in green bower,
To be king of the bone and the blood,

To be priest in the tabernacle
Of the turf and holy seed,

To defy the coming of rooks' covens
That will whirl winters round my rimed head

Who lay seven years of her kingdom
Emperor and in thrall,

Despite all to be struck down from faithless
Time's tower in the end,

True to the end remaining
To the one love, ineluctable.

What Do I Breathe for Now?

What do I breathe for now?
Older by a day
Than that wastrel folly
Moon-drowned a dark ago,
What have I to show?

    Instinct knits my bones together,
    Hunger stuffs my skin,
    Time and terror make the weather
    We do loving in.
    The weather near us bleakens
    The green light on the ground
    Where we spend the seeking seed
    And plummet deep as need.

What wisdom do we reach
Who draw another breath,
What grace of act or speech
Escapes to us from death?
We linger in the light.

    The animal fretwork of the veins,
    The involuntary flow,
    The bellying moon that swells and wanes,
    The long cockerel's cockcrow,
    The unintelligent senses sing
    In single choir together.
    Love wrests the weather of delight
    From our breath against the night.

As I was Going to Saint-Ives

As I was going to Saint-Ives
In stormy, windy, sunny weather
I met a man with seven wives
(The herons stand in the swift water).

One drinks her beer out of his can
In stormy, windy, and bright weather,
And who laughs more, she or her man?
(The herons stand still on the water.)

One knows the room his candle lit
In stormy, lightning, cloudburst weather,
That glows again at the thought of it
(Two herons still the swift water).

His jealous, wild-tongued, Wednesday's wife—
In dreepy, wintry, wind-lashed weather
—What's better than that ranting strife?
(Two herons still the roaring water.)

There's one whose mind's so like his mind
In streaming wind or balmy weather
All joy, all wisdom seem one kind.
(The herons stand in the swift water.)

And one whose secret mazes he
In moon-swept, in torrential weather
Ransacks, and cannot find the key
(Two herons stand in the white water).

He'll think of none save one's slim thighs
In heat and sleet and windy weather
Till death has plucked his dreaming eyes
(Two herons guard the streaming water).

And when to Saint-Ives then I came
In fairest, windiest, rainiest weather,
They called his shadow by my name.
(The herons stand in the quick water.)

And the one whose love moves all he's done,
In windy, warm, and wintry weather,
—What can he leave but speaks thereon?
(Two herons still the swift water.)